Life After Death

Life After Death

What Happens Next?

Jeffrey D. Johnson

WIPF & STOCK · Eugene, Oregon

LIFE AFTER DEATH
What Happens Next?

Wipf & Stock
An Imprint of Wipf and Stock Publishers
199 W. 8th Ave., Suite 3
Eugene, OR 97401
www.wipfandstock.com

ISBN 13: 978-1-61097-110-2

Manufactured in the U.S.A.

Dedicated to Grandma Johnson! You loved Jesus, life and you loved me. You showed me how to live and taught me about the hope of eternity in Christ Jesus. I look so forward to hugging you once again—and having red Jello with you in Heaven.

EVERYONE WILL face the loss of a loved one in their life, and everyone will experience the loss of their own life. What happens when death occurs? Will I see my loved one again? Will I continue to live in another dimension? What comes after death? Is there a heaven (most people in the world believe in Heaven)? What does heaven mean?

Final Destination

According to the Bible, the final destination of all believers is the New Heaven and New Earth as recorded for us in Revelation 21. This is not some fluffy, cloudy place, filled with strumming harps and people singing homogenous songs of ecstasy. Rather, it is a real place, in real time, with real people and celestial beings.

Trust

We can trust what God's Word states regarding the afterlife. We know we will be with loved ones. We know we will be with God. We know God has a plan. We know that eternity is beyond anything we could ever imagine. We know that the beauty and awesomeness will be profound regardless of how mind-numbing Hollywood has made Heaven to be.

Number of Days (Psa. 139:16)

Living to be 70 years old, one will experience 25,550 mornings. Seems like a long time, doesn't it? But over the years, a person begins to realize how swift, how precious, and how fragile each day really is. Knowing these things, we should in some form create a point of reference. For the atheist, these 25,550 mornings are a countdown to nothingness, to oblivion. The agnostic hopes for an afterlife—a "we'll see after the last breath" attitude. Concerning the afterlife, the apostle John writes, "Beloved, now we are children of God; and it has not yet been revealed what we shall be, but we know that when he is revealed, we shall be like him, for we shall see him as he is" (1 John 3:2). The point of reference for the apostle is that of an eternity with God in Christ.

Creeds

The Nicene Creed states, "And we look for the resurrection of the dead, and the life of the world to come." The Apostle's Creed records, "I believe . . . in the resurrection of the body, and the life everlasting." From the beginning, Christians looked forward to life everlasting. There have been several books written about what Heaven would be like; however, much of Heaven remains a mystery—and mystery is good, for "eye has not seen, nor ear heard, nor have entered into the heart of man the things which God has prepared for those who love him" (1 Cor. 2:9).

Gnostics

One reason that people believe that Heaven will be a boring experience is connected with the ancient Gnostic teaching that everything physical is evil and everything spiritual is good. To believe the Gnostics is to misunderstand the biblical teaching regarding God's creation. God called his creation "very good" (Gen. 1:31). Sin, however, has changed the dynamic of universe and the status of human beings' relationship with God. God has promised to renew all things both physical and spiritual (Rev. 21). Jesus came to pay the penalty for sin, and the whole of creation is waiting for redemption (Rom. 8).

Glimpses

We have a glimpse of Heaven in stories of profound love found between people; people and pets; in the most beautiful, awe-inspiring places on earth, or in the multitudinous glories of the universe; in the joy that a baby brings to the parents and grandparents. Any experience that is good and beautiful, any that is safe or warm, loving and kind, anything you can imagine that can be summarized as good and joyful, is only a glimpse of Heaven (James 1:17).

Raising All Things

Jesus said, "This is the will of the Father who sent me, that of all he has given me I should lose nothing, but should raise it up at the last day" (John 6:39).

The Greek word, translated "it," is a neuter pronoun meaning that that Jesus will raise not only people but all things created (Rom. 8:19–22; Col. 1:20).

Everything Good

Everything good will continue: the physicality of every creature; everything emotional; everything we sense on the earth and in the universe from breezes, fragrances, light, and aliveness. There will be work, learning, sciences, arts, everything enjoyable (Gen. 2:15; 1 Cor. 13:12; Rev. 14:2, 3). God loves his creation and proclaimed it good, and creation itself is a mirror of God's magnificence and glory (Gen. 1:31; Psa. 19). Therefore, it is only natural to think that the renewal of creation will be part of our appreciation and activity of enjoyment in the afterlife.

Everything Bad

What will no longer be in existence is evil, sin, anything that is emotionally negative or physically harmful. No death, sadness, hunger, nothing representative of destruction, impairment, or mischief. No ecological damage, no mental illness, no pain, no grief.

Our emotions, which are very much part being human, will experience a greater dimension of expression without the baggage of anything negative, painful, or sorrowful. Imagine only joy, compassion, and love. Imagine a fulfillment with complete gratification of experience and much, much more.

Mystery

Some things remain a mystery regarding Heaven—and that is okay. Heaven is more than anything we could ever imagine. This paper does not attempt to address all the incredible details about the afterlife, nor does it grapple with the various interpretations of God's judgment(s), resurrections(s)[1], and all things future. However, there are a few colossal components we *do* know regarding what happens after our last breath. And with these we begin:

1. INTERMEDIATE STATE

The idea of the intermediate state is that we have complete consciousness after death (Eccl. 12:7; Luke 16:22–24). Between death and the resurrection of the body, something happens. Jesus said to the thief on the cross that at the moment of death he would be with him in Paradise (Luke 23:43). The intermediate state is the condition of any individual, believer and nonbeliever, immediately after death. A glimpse of this is found in Luke 16: 22, where Jesus tells the story of a man who died and was with Abraham and of a man who died and was in torment. In this story, you find conversation and consciousness which defines the reality of continuing existence after death.

Paul stated that to absent from the body (death) means that we will be present with the Lord (2 Cor. 5:8). There is no "soul sleep," as some interpret the Christian euphemism of "sleep" as found in 1 Corinthians 11:30 and 15:51. The word "sleep" simply refers to death. The body looks as though it is sleeping. The spirit has departed from our body, thus ending our life here on earth. The bodily part of us appears to "sleep" until the final resurrection.

Meanwhile, the spiritual part of us transfers to a conscious state of existence before the Lord. Apparently, this conscious state has some form of physicality, a form that is descriptive and recognizable. The book of Revelation is replete with descriptions of individuals who have previously died being in a physical context before the final resurrection takes place (Rev. 6:9, 10; 7:10; 8:6, 13). The book of Hebrews also points to physical descriptions of individuals in the intermediated state (Heb. 8:5; 12:22–23). It is clear that there will be a "spirit-type" of body between death and the final resurrection. The description is that of people wearing clothes, crowns, holding branches, and having body parts.

This place is not what Catholics refer to as Purgatory. The belief in Purgatory developed during the Middle Ages and became Catholic dogma at the Council of Trent (1545–1563) as a reaction to the Protestant rejection of the teaching. One will not find the concept of Purgatory in the Bible—only in the Apocrypha (2 Macc. 12:43–45).

Though much is speculation regarding the intermediate state; it doesn't, however, diminish the certainty of the hope of the *parousia* (Gr. "Second Coming" or "presence") of Christ in a new creation! After death, believers will experience Christ's presence (1 John 3:2–3) and, ultimately, the resurrection of their body to enjoy the New Heaven and New Earth.

2. CHRIST WILL RETURN

According to Christ's answers to the apostle's questions as to what will be the sign of his coming and the end of the age, we find a decline in civilization rather than evolutionary buoyancy. Disasters in nature, horrid warfare, a redefinition of Christianity that leads to apostasy, and global human despair is found in Christ's description of world history leading up to the second coming (Matt. 24:3–27). Within this construct of time, a nefarious personality called the "the man of sin" (2 Thess. 2:3–4) or Antichrist will eventually hold the world in his sway until the Second Coming of Christ. At the Second Coming, Christ will not appear in a quiet little town in the West Bank; he will come on the clouds of Heaven (Matt. 26:64), and in so doing crush the reign of the Antichrist. History will be altered once again because of this man from Galilee. The divine will reign supreme in the affairs of humankind.

It is not known when Christ will return (Acts 1:7). We know he will come as an unexpected thief (1 Thess. 5:2). We are to always be prepared for his coming, always expecting him to arrive. We are to "watch" for him (Mark 13:37). Therefore, we understand that his coming is *imminent*—it is always near, and there is always a tension of expectancy.[2]

3. OUR BODIES WILL BE RESURRECTED

We not only believe in the immortality of the soul but that one day our immortal souls will be reunited with our resurrected bodies—for the lover of God, a resurrection entering into eternal bliss, and for the rejecter of God, a resurrection into eternal darkness.

At the resurrection, every part of our body will be raised, and not one hair will perish (Luke 21:18). The resurrection body is said to be a spiritual body (1 Cor. 15:35–46). This simply means our bodies will be released from the chains of a sinful-fallen state into a celestial existence. We will have the same qualities of

Christ's human body on the Mount of Transfiguration and after his resurrection.

We will be recognizable, as our corruptible must put on incorruption (1 Cor. 15:53), as this form passes away (1 Cor. 7:31), and we become eternally new—never growing old, without sickness, without pain, and without sorrow (Rev. 21:1–5). Just as Mary recognized the resurrected Jesus' voice, our voice will also be recognized. Just as the disciples knew Jesus by the way he did things (folded the napkin, threw the net on the other side, saying a blessing in Emmaus), so it is that we will be recognized by our loved ones because of the little idiosyncrasies we manifest in Heaven. Jesus said of his resurrected body, "Behold my hands and my feet, that it is I myself; handle me, and see, for a spirit does not have flesh and bones as you see I have" (Luke 24:39). "Handle me" suggests embrace. What an incredible moment that will be when we experience the celestial reunion of people we love.

4. THERE WILL BE A KINGDOM

Though Christ's Kingdom is beyond our full comprehension, we do understand a few details.

First, it will be not be homogeneous. Within the kingdom, one will find diversity, the opposite of sameness. Like the Body of Christ today exemplifies an assortment of peoples, talents, and abilities, so it will be true in the kingdom. God will give each of us a "name" that only we will know (Rev. 2:17). The Lord will bestow upon all both great and small responsibility and rest. There will be different rooms in God's house for his servants (John 14:2), which speaks of activity and special work in the Kingdom. Just as there are servants with different statuses and work in kingdoms and governments today, so shall it be in the thousand-year reign of Christ (Rev. 20:4–6).

Second, there will be life to the fullest. The Kingdom (and the New Heaven and New Earth which follow) shall not be a reclaiming of the original Eden as much as it will be a restoring and renovation—simply a renewed beginning, something that is greater than the first. God is infinite, implying a movement, not stagnation; rather, a moving forward, constantly unfolding. Our souls belong to God, and in the Kingdom we will still seek him. We will be in his presence and yet He will be "Other"; we will bask in his glory and yet still have the need to grow; we will find rest and still be pilgrims; we will sit at his feet and still find mystery. As God continually unfolds and reveals himself to us, we also continue to move straight ahead "from glory to glory" (2 Cor. 3:18), meaning that the Christian experiences justification (forgiveness of sin), sanctification (living like Christ [Gal. 5:22–25]), and glorification (being in our resurrected body in his presence). However, we will never completely comprehend God; we will never exhaust his reality; we will forever be learning, ever growing in an eternity of God revealing himself to us. Our journey will never cease. We will be more alive than ever before, beyond anything we could ever imagine.

5. OUR WORKS WILL FOLLOW US IN THE AFTERLIFE (REV. 14:13)

The word "rest" has the idea of freedom from weakness, failure, and the limitations we currently have in our body. In other words, we shall continue to be productive without the fragility of becoming tired, or pausing, reinforcing the principle of moving straight ahead, that of progressive activity. Christ tells us that there will be the reward of more responsibility and gratification of self-worth (Matt. 24:45–47; 25:20–23; Luke 19:15–19). To the great will be given great and to the small will be given small—all will have worth and responsibility within the Kingdom, meaning that our life-work here is a preparation for bigger, ongoing work there.

Jesus is our Shepherd and we will be like him. He has given us a paradigm to understand. The Scripture states that Jesus is the same in the past as he is today and as he will be in the future (Hebrews 13:8). This being true, we can understand the principle in this manner: Jesus is the same yesterday, for he was the creator of the universe and all therein before he became flesh in Bethlehem. Jesus is the same today, for on earth he was a carpenter, someone who works for others. He worked long hard hours. In Heaven, he intercedes for us, being the head, the chief cornerstone of the church, and he is our Savior. Jesus is the same forever, as he will be the ruler, the king over his kingdom of multitudinous, busy, laboring, serving, co-reigning redeemed people. Jesus puts it plainly when he states, "My Father has been working until now and I have been working" (John 5:17). He also said, "I say to you, he who believes in me, the works that I do he will do also; and greater works than these he will do" (John 14:12).

6. WE WILL BE ACTIVELY ENGAGED IN LIFE IN THE KINGDOM

a. Making decisions and interfacing with people (Matt. 19:28; 1 Cor. 6:2)

A judge, in a biblical construct, is a representative or ambassador of a nation, kingdom, tribe, or empire. Such a one travels and interfaces with other people, making decisions and altering the course of events. The implication is profound as one ponders that the One we are representing is the Creator of the universe and all things that exist. Our travels will be filled with splendid views and experiences of all things God has made. You've seen the glorious Hubble Telescope photos? You will experience the universe with all your senses fully engaged, wide-eyed with 100 percent adrenaline. You will discover lifeforms and beauty that presently we can only imagine. Oh, the wonder of it all!

b. Dealing and conversing with angels (1 Cor. 6:3)

Think of it: We will be communicating with the vast, innumerable variety of multitudinous celestial beings that are ever-present before the Throne of God who have done God's bidding for millennia. We will know these glorious beings who protected Israel and the saints down through the ages. We will learn of the particulars of how angels protected us in our life's journey. We will begin to understand the events surrounding eternity past and the mind of God as told by the Seraphim, Cherubim, Archangels, and Angels. Incredible!

c. Assignments according to our love for the Master (2 Tim. 2:11, 12; Rev. 5:10; Luke 19; Matt. 25)

To the degree we identified ourselves with Christ here and now will be the degree of our eternal assignments. If we are faithful in little things, God will reward us with greater things. To honor the Lord with our "substance" (which generally refers to goods, assets, or money) was understood or commonly interpreted as meaning grace that was given by God, or to honor the Lord because of his love towards us. The motivation surrounding our love for God is predicated by God's love for us (1 John 4:19). God will honor those who fear him (Psa. 111:5) with a single portion but will give a greater portion to those who are driven by love.

Paul stated that one should be strong in "grace" (2 Tim 2:1) and that if we "die with him" we shall also "live with him" (2 Tim. 2:11, 12), meaning that our lives should be completely consumed and identified with Christ. A spouse will willingly give their life, give their all, for their husband/wife not because they fear them, but rather because they love them. When a person loves another person that one will be motivated to do more, to invest in the person they love. In turn, they will receive blessing. So it was in the parable of the talents. Those who loved their master invested according to their ability and at the end of the day, and when their lord returned, they received a greater blessing for their expression of love. However, the one who was afraid of his master, choosing to be overly cautious—paralyzed with fear, thus not moving forward and not willing to invest his time or ability received little—received nothing (Matt. 25:14–30). So will it be in the Kingdom of Heaven. The reward will be measured by our love, not our fear.

7. RENEWED GLORY

The New Heaven, New Earth, and New Jerusalem are the finally redeemed universe (Isa. 65:17; 66:22; Matt. 19:28; Acts 3:21; Rom. 8:18–21; 2 Pet. 3:13; Rev. 21:1–8). Isaiah, Jesus, Peter, Paul, and John address the renewed universe giving hope to all of God's creation.

Two Greek words for new: *Neos* is something that did not exist before, therefore is new. *Kainos* is something that does exist; however, it has changed. It is better, it is greater than before. It is enhanced, it is superior; therefore, it is renewed, and its quality has changed for the better. Like that of a person who believes in Christ becomes a "new man" (Eph. 4:24, *Kainos*), the quality of the person has become better and has become new. *Kainos* is used for the New Heavens and New Earth and New Jerusalem in Revelation 21. Isaiah uses a similar Hebrew word (*Chadash*) in chapter 65:17 and 66:22. Simply stated, the universe will be renewed, renovated into a better or improved place.

In this divinely renewed universe, we will experience things beyond our finest imaginings, and all things that were mentioned regarding the kingdom and things experientially immeasurable and incomprehensible will fully bloom in this renewed environment of creation. An eternity of discovery, a continuing of God's unveiling mysteries and wonders; a forever learning, growing, joyous existence of understanding truth, and meaning; never boring, never redundant, completely stimulating, always fulfilling, will be what God has prepared for those who love him.

FINAL THOUGHTS AND SUMMARY ABOUT WHAT WE KNOW ABOUT THE AFTERLIFE

1. God will take care of you (Psa. 34:6; 91:4; Isa. 25:4; Rom. 8:37–39).
2. After our last breath, we experience consciousness in a spirit-body that has a recognized form. Believers will be in the presence of God; nonbelievers will be in torment (Luke 16:19–31).
3. Christ will return and change the current state of humanity, bringing universal peace, harmony, and justice, undoing the harness of lawlessness and evil.
4. Our bodies will be resurrected into a super-body, a glorified body similar to Christ's resurrected body. We will recognize each other and those who have gone on before us in death. Our actual bodies will come alive without the weaknesses and flaws we currently have, for we will be new and strong, healthy and no longer tired (Job 19:25–27).
5. There will be a kingdom—"Thy Kingdom come" (Matt. 6:10). Within this kingdom, there will be tasks to be assigned, responsibilities to be handled. There will be activity and movement as people work together seeking God living life to the fullest imagination. There will be animals in the kingdom—this would imply pets (Isa. 65:25).
6. We will be able to continue our work and fulfill our heart's desire (Rev. 14:13). We will finally be free from limitations that hold us back from fleshing out our full potential. We will be able to experience great accomplishment in the afterlife (John 14:12). Paul implies in Colossians 3:23 and 24 that we will continue with our talents and gifts as an act of worship to the Lord. Painters, scientists, musicians, athletes, carpenters, and so forth will find uninhibited fulfillment and joy in their gifted areas of expertise.

We will eventually reside in a renewed version of the earth and universe. A beauty that is beyond present imagination; a forever stimulating experience of discovery and purpose, with God in Christ being the central focal point. To live in blissful rapture, ever learning, ever moving, ever growing, everlasting. This is our future!

"*For to me, to live is Christ, and to die is gain*"
(Phil. 1:21).

Bibliography

Ahlquist, Diane, *The Complete Idiot's Guide to Life After Death*, Alpha Books, 2007

Alcorn, Randy, *Heaven*, Tyndale House Publishers, Inc., 2004

Criswell, W. A., *Expository Sermons on Revelation*, Criswell Publishing, 1995

Elwell, Walter A., *Evangelical Dictionary of Theology*, Baker Book House, 1984

Galan, Benjamin, *What's So Great About Heaven*, Rose Publishing, 2009

House & Price, *Charts of Bible Prophecy*, Zondervan, 2003

LaHaye & Ice, *Charting the End Times*, Harvest House Publishers, 2001

Lockyer, Hebert, *All About the Second Coming*, Hendrickson Publishers, 1997

New King James Version, The Holy Bible, Thomas Nelson, Inc., 1982

Pentecost, J. Dwight, Things to Come, Zondervan, 1981

Robertson, A.T., *Word Pictures in the New Testament*, Holman Bible Publishers, 2000

Segal, Alan F., *Life After Death*, Doubleday, 2004

Stern, David H., *Jewish New Testament Commentary*, Jewish New Testament Publications, Inc., 1992

Walvoord & Zuck, *The Bible Knowledge Commentary*, Victor Books, 1987

Ware, Bishop Kallistos, *The Orthodox Way*, St. Vladimir's Seminary Press, 1995

Young, Brad H., The Parables, Jewish Tradition and Christian Interpretation, Hendrickson Publishers, 1998

Endnotes

1. Enoch & Elijah did not die, however, were translated (Gen. 5:24; 2 Kg. 2:11) and some believe they are to be the two witnesses of Revelation 11:1, 2 who will die and be resurrected. Some OT saints were resurrected (Matt. 27:51, 52). Some Church saints were resurrected (Acts 9:36-41; 14:19-20; 20:9-10). There is the resurrection of Christ (1 Cor. 15:20, 23); Resurrection of Life (Jn. 5:29); Resurrection of the Condemned (Jn. 5:29); More Church saints resurrected (1 Thess. 4:13-18, referred to as the "Rapture"); All OT saints resurrected (Rev. 20:4); Resurrection of the Wicked (Rev. 20:12-13); Judgment of Living Jews and Gentiles (Ezek. 20:33-39; Matt. 25:31-46); Great White Throne Judgment (Dan. 12:2; Jn. 5:29; Rev. 20:11-15); Judgment of Satan and Wicked (Rev. 20:14-15); and the Judgment Seat of Christ (2 Cor. 5:10; Rom. 14:10; 1 Cor. 3:11-15). For complete information regarding God's judgments and the resurrections see: *Things to Come*, J. Dwight Pentecost, Zondervan Publishing House, 1981.

2. For more information regarding the various views on the Second Coming of Christ see: *Charting the End Times*, Time LaHaye & Thomas Ice, Harvest House Publishers, 2001.